spiral with me

Jennifer Finelli

spiral with me © 2023 Jennifer Finelli

All rights reserved.

No part of this publication may be reproduced, stored in a retrieval system, or transmitted, in any form or by any means, electronic, mechanical, photocopying, recording, or otherwise, without the prior written permission of the presenters.

Jennifer Finelli asserts the moral right to be identified as the author of this work.

Presentation by *BookLeaf Publishing*

Web: www.bookleafpub.com

E-mail: info@bookleafpub.com

ISBN: 9789357743686

First edition 2023

DEDICATION

To myself. For finally having the courage to take my thoughts beyond the notebooks under my bed.

ACKNOWLEDGEMENT

I'd like to acknowledge my mother, for supporting my dreams in that stairwell when I needed it most.

Do You Feel It Too

Do you ever get tired of being that girl
Who closes her eyes to turn off the world
Who lives in a world inside of her head
And is afraid to bring dreams outside of her bed
The girl who makes herself smaller to fit in a mold
Instead of accepting herself as none other than bold
The girl who's afraid to take up space and own her positions
Who thinks people's opinions mean more than her own intuitions
The girl who simply and truly holds herself back
Unwilling to present herself to the world without achievements pre-stacked

And you get so mad at yourself, you want to be different

And you can't help but feel your self-sabotage is deliberate

Isn't It Sad

They teach you how to treat others, but never yourself
And more often than not, your thoughts are meaner to you than anyone else

Cosmic

The sun goes down for the moon to come up;
Everyone assuming it's sacrificial for love

But when you put me down to bring others up,
It feels like nothing I do is ever enough

My Deepest Fear

When you look at me for too long
I'm scared your perception of me will grow clearer
That you will take a long look at me
And you'll see what I do when I look in the mirror
A girl who is not quite as pretty
As the ones in the magazines
The girl who has a little extra stomach
Hanging over her jeans
A girl who doesn't particularly have a talent
Who just paddles to stay afloat
A girl who doesn't have many achievements worthy to note
I'm scared when your eyes linger for a second longer than normal
You won't see me as a diamond in the rough
I'm scared you simply will see me as nowhere near enough

Tired Soldier

I give my warmest hug
to try and thaw the ice
I over-explain my love
to try and play nice
If I had a white flag I'd wave it
I face the storm and brave it
You tell me the weather's fine
It's my fault the hurricane started in my mind

Agoraphobic

I feel safe, when I'm laying in bed
When I'm in my apartment
And the doubtful thoughts are just in my head
Nothing bad happens, when you are laying in bed
You don't get filled with the same existential dread
You're in control of what happens, when you're laying in bed
You don't have to tip-toe around and lightly tread
You don't have to worry, when you are laying in bed
Because no one can hurt you and you won't be misled
You miss a lot of moments, when you are laying in bed
And a lot of good thoughts end up going unsaid
You try and work up the courage to get out of bed
But you panic, and lay back down instead

Blindsided

The Ocean grabs a hold of you
Calm and still as can be
Gently gaining your comfort as you slowly inch up your feet
The sun singes your forehead while you close your eyes and breathe
Before you can exhale
The sand disappears below your feet
The waves start crashing
The sky turns a charcoal grey
Your body is thrashing as the waves take you away
In one unpredictable second your peace and comfort went astray
I would rather get blindsided by the Ocean, than I would by you any day

My Father

Like a pine tree, standing tall within a crowd
No matter how strong the gust of wind, his feet
are firmly in the ground
Like the cabin in the forest
Protected by the tree
My father never lets anything blow me off my
feet
I look up to my father like you look up to a tree
Taking in his strength, someone you aspire to
one day be

Self Preservation

I see the way they make fun of people
who do what I do
I can't shake the feeling
that they will talk behind my back too

The Spiral

The hands move on a clock someone told us to set
There's another tragedy on the news that I will never get
There's something about your 20s that makes you question your self-worth
And with the state of the world, what could possibly be my purpose
You think when you are younger you are bound to make a difference
But as each year goes by you learn, your inflated importance was
Clouded by ignorance
Every once in a while, I try and stomach the humbling notion
That I'm one of 7 billion just going through the motions

Burn Out

And after all this time, my
Legs are starting to crumble from this weight
You added one too many burdens
And my sanity is at stake
You knew I could handle a challenge
But at what cost
I can't help but feel
I was set up for an imbalanced loss
I hide in the bathroom because I can't hold back
my tears
I think about addressing it and your
Curtness amplifies my fears
I add another boulder to the overflowing pile
The casualty doesn't count for you when
It's just my stability and pride

TW: SA// He Said// She Said

Boys will be boys they say in defense.
He handed her a drink, his hand moved up her dress
She reached for her friends, her arms feeling heavy
He swooped in, saved the day, keeping her steady
No one questioned the hero, taking her home;
A good guy, who couldn't let her go on her own
He bought her a drink; of course, before she was near
And they automatically assumed she couldn't handle a beer
Her consciousness fading, but she could hear the yells
His friends were catching up, and quickly she could tell
One hero wouldn't suffice; they all wanted the glory
And her dignity wasn't stolen in their version of the story

Patience

They told me to be patient
That I don't need to rush
In case they didn't tell you, time's a helpful crux
I would wait and wait and wait, but no one seemed to notice
And now that I'm grown up
When I wait I lose all focus
It's not that I'm impatient, although they'll try and say that's true
But when you spend a lifetime waiting
Your view of the world becomes skewed
It's not for lack of trying, that I truly know
But when life would rear its ugly head
Progress would plateau
Despite its importance, or relevance to me
It was pushed to the back burner, it seemed to always be
I naively always hoped that this time would be different
That I wouldn't add another bullet point to the list of things unfinished
Now at 25, if I have to wait I tremble
If I'm not in control
I'll simply have a meltdown
Everyone always argues

Nature vs. Nurture
Sometimes I wonder if I'd be the same
If patience hadn't been self-torture

Range

Yesterday I was happy
Today I was chillingly sad
Tomorrow my biggest accomplishment
Might be getting out of bed
I don't think anyone realizes
The power words play
And when you ask me why I'm worrying so much
I think I've bothered you all day
I can't help these thoughts
But nobody seems to believe it
I don't accept I've locked my door until I take
A picture to peek at
I triple check the number before I send a text
I'm constantly terrified of what might happen next
If only life had a script, of each and every play
It would bring me immense comfort all throughout the day
I try to remind myself
To live in the moment
But uncertainty has always been my biggest opponent

The Cycle

Time and time again
They are nice to you in private
But once you're in a crowd
Their respect for you turns silent
They say it doesn't matter
But it matters to me
The way someone is treated
Shouldn't be wrapped in inconsistency

The Second Shift

I wake up, stumbling over the piles of clothes on the floor
After work... I promise myself... another lie I naively fall for
I pass the sink... dishes to be cleaned, garbage to be taken out
More responsibilities I need to care about
Skip breakfast, out in a rush
First meal of the day way past lunch
I don't have time to be hungry or tired
Functioning on pure stress and anxiety
Can't breathe all day, scrambling on eggshells
Any moment now will bring echoes of misplaced yells
Past dinner time, I finally come home
It's dark and for the first time all day I'm alone
My hand in the chip bag I sit and sigh
Dinner seems to be my only me time
I trip over the same clothes on the floor,
This time, adding one more
I'll wake up early before work, I say to myself yawning
The prospect of the cycle continuing tomorrow, daunting

For My Mother

When I look at you, I see an abundance of strength
And when you look in the mirror, I wish you would see the same
A mother who carries pain that isn't her own
To make her children not feel alone
And when you look in the mirror I wish you would see
The years of laughter and memories
Wrinkles tell a story of a life that was worth living
And I love the way yours fold around your eyes when you are reminiscing
I wish you would see the growth and forgiveness in your eyes
And the way that time has melded you to be nothing other than wise
And when you look in the mirror and don't feel like yourself
I hope you see me in your eyes and the shape of your face
And know that I hold our similarities proudly, with grace
The beauty within me came from the beauty within you
And when you look in the mirror, I hope you see that too

Burn Out Part II

Another load on my back,
So, they don't have to carry it
Another bullet on my dart board,
A win to give my adversaries

To My Younger Self

Your worth is not determined
By the opinions of others
The thoughts of other people, shouldn't let you suffer
If only you would believe that
There's so much peace you would discover
You will be the bad guy in someone's version of the story
Not everyone will like you, but you will recover

Ode to Tiger Part I

For the first time in my life, I'm struck with this indelible feeling
Like the unconditional love I had known before, Held underlying conditional meaning
To everyone before you, I served some kind of purpose
And if I didn't oblige, I was made to be known I was worthless
When you hear it so many times, from so many different people
It plants the seed in your head, you think your worthlessness is believable
It's hard to forget how you were treated in the past, poison tends to linger
But your patience when I doubt myself
Softens the blow of my triggers
You once told me scars were stories, and boy do I have plenty
Not everyone in my lifetime has treated me quite as gently
I knew it the moment I met you, as crazy as it seems
You started as my person, and that's what you will forever be

Ode to Tiger Part II

When you look in the mirror
I hope they smile back
I hope you tell them
Life has not just one set track
I hope you think a little clearer
About all that you have done
I hope you know that growth looks different for everyone
Your worth is not dependent on what you can or can't achieve
You have so much within you and within your very reach
And when you feel your dignity slipping through the cracks
I hope you treat yourself gently, please cut yourself some slack
You don't have to be perfect
To deserve love and respect
Mistakes are part of being human
And respect is part of that

Printed in the USA
CPSIA information can be obtained
at www.ICGtesting.com
LVHW020906051223
765518LV00087B/2954